Postcard History Series

Lighthouses of the Southern Atlantic and Gulf States

LIGHTHOUSE TOWER. The painting and design of the lighthouse tower and keepers' quarters allow sailors to easily identify individual stations during daylight hours, when the light and fog signals were not operating. Day shapes or daymarks are mast head signals comprised of geometric shapes. The four basic shapes of the marks are ball, cylinder, cone, and diamond, and many times, there is a solid color or split color combination. (Author's collection.)

ON FRONT COVER: ST. MARKS LIGHT STATION. St. Marks Light Station is the oldest light station in Florida, constructed in 1831 at the mouth of the St. Mark River on Apalachee Bay. (Author's collection.)

ON BACK COVER: NEW CANAL LIGHTHOUSE. The New Canal Lighthouse is where the Confederate forces kept the light active until New Orleans fell to the Union forces in April 1862. (Author's collection.)

POSTCARD HISTORY SERIES

Lighthouses of the Southern Atlantic and Gulf States

Linda Osborne Cynowa

ISBN 978-1-4671-6259-3

Published by Arcadia Publishing
Charleston, South Carolina

Printed in the United States of America

Library of Congress Control Number: 2024951739

For all general information contact Arcadia Publishing at:
Telephone 843-853-2070
Fax 843-853-0044
E-mail sales@arcadiapublishing.com

Visit us on the Internet at www.arcadiapublishing.com

This book is dedicated to all the historians and archivists who work so hard to keep the many pieces of our past safe for future generations. And to the lighthouse keepers, both men and women, who maintained the lights in the lonely conditions and helped keep the lakes and seas as safe as possible for maritime navigation.

Contents

Acknowledgments

I would like to thank the many places where information on these important lights can be obtained: North Point Range Lighthouse, Cobb Point Bar Lighthouse for the Chesapeake Chapter US Lighthouse Society (USLS), Friends of the Fenwick Island Lighthouse, Friends of Concord Point Lighthouse, Cove Point Lighthouse, Drum Point Lighthouse with the Calvert Marine Museum Society, Chesapeake Bay Maritime Museum–Hooper Strait Lighthouse, Old Point Comfort Lighthouse, Mathews County Historical Society–New Point Comfort Lighthouse, Assateague Lighthouse, Windmill Point Lighthouse, Deepwater Shoals Lighthouse, Old Plantation Lighthouse, Thimble Shoals Lighthouse, Jones Point Lighthouse, Jordon Point Lighthouse, Old Cape Henry Lighthouse, New Cape Henry Lighthouse, Cap Charles Lighthouse, Cape Hatteras Lighthouse, Currituck Beach Lighthouse, Cape Lookout Lighthouse, Bodie Island Lighthouse, Ocracoke Lighthouse, Edenton Historical Commission for Roanoke River Light, Diamond Shoals Lighthouse, Old Baldy Foundation for Bald Head Lighthouse, Price's Creek Lighthouse, Morris Island Lighthouse, Friends of the Hunting Island Lighthouse, Fort Sumter Lighthouse, Georgetown Lighthouse, Cape Roman Lighthouse, Tybee Island Lighthouse, Sapelo Island Lighthouse, St. Simons Island Lighthouse, Cockspur Island Lighthouse, Little Cumberland Island Lighthouse, Tybee Knoll Cut Range Lighthouse, Amelia Island Lighthouse, Key West Lighthouse, Cape Florida Lighthouse, Jupiter Inlet Lighthouse, Cape Canaveral Lighthouse, St. Augustine Lighthouse, Hillsboro Inlet Lighthouse, Ponce de Leon Inlet Lighthouse, Fowey Rocks Lighthouse, Sand Key Lighthouse, Sanibel Island Lighthouse, Port Boca Grande Lighthouse, Gasparilla Island Light, Anclote Keys Lighthouse, Crooked River Lighthouse, St. Marks Lighthouse, Egmont Key Lighthouse, Cape St. George Lighthouse, Cape San Blas Lighthouse, Choctaw Lighthouse, Battery Gladden Lighthouse, Mobile Bay Lighthouse, Sand Island Lighthouse, Mobile Bay Range Lighthouses, Cat Island Lighthouse, Ship Island Lighthouse, Biloxi Lighthouse, Merrill Shell Bank Lighthouse, Merrill's Shell Bank Lighthouse, Sabine Pass Lighthouse, New Canal Lighthouse, Port Pontchartrain Lighthouse, Point Au For Reef Lighthouse, West Rigolets Lighthouse, Cubits Gap Lighthouse, Point Isabel, Lighthouse, Bolivar point Lighthouse, Brazos Santiago Lighthouse, Half Moon Reef Lighthouse, Brazos River Lighthouse, Galveston Getty Lighthouse. Fort Point Lighthouse, and Redfish Bar Lighthouse.

A grateful thank-you goes to the US Department of Homeland Security, the US Coast Guard, and the US National Archives. I would also like to thank *Lighthouse Digest* magazine.

For further information on these important beacons of navigation, look into the many well-written and informative books by Jeremy D'Entremont.

All postcards used, unless otherwise credited, are the property of the author. You can contact the author through the website lindaosborecynowa.com for more information.

Introduction

The lighthouses along the Southern Atlantic and Gulf Coast states have a variety of different characteristics than you might find along the Pacific coast, northern coast, or even in the Great Lakes area. The uses of the lighthouses have always been the same: directing mariners to safe harbors and ships away from dangerous reefs and shoals. With their different shapes and styles, some tall and many shorter in stature, they all have a job to do. The states included in the Southern Atlantic and Gulf coasts include Maryland, Virginia, North and South Carolina, Georgia, Florida, Alabama, Mississippi, Louisiana, and Texas. These states have different situations to deal with along with the more natural maritime concerns than lights elsewhere would experience.

During the Civil War, at the early start of the conflict, the state of Virginia and the Florida Keys remained in the hands of the Union. Both Union and Confederate forces fought to retain control of the more than 160 lighthouses in the southern states. The Union forces wanted control of the lighthouses to help with naval operations and to be able to get troops and supplies to the frontline coastal sites. For the Confederate forces, the need to hinder the Union forces became of paramount concern because of the dangerous nighttime navigation that took place. Watching the movements of both naval and land forces became important for both sides. The US Lighthouse Service did assist the Union effort throughout the war by relighting many of the lighthouses where the lens had been extinguished or removed by the Confederate forces. When the war was over, the USLS needed 10 years to relight and refurbish the hundreds of southern lighthouses to their prewar condition.

Weather is always a concern with the prevalence of hurricanes that have hit these areas so frequently over the many years that lighthouses have been in service. Many times, the lighthouses have been used to shelter people from the area when the weather turned violent, often saving many lives. In 1992, Hurricane Andrew eroded a major part of the beach area around the Cape St. George Lighthouse, and the Coast Guard, in 1994, deactivated the light out of concern for its stability. Then Hurricane Opal struck in 1995, and the tidal surge pulled it off its foundation, where it tilted and settled into the sand. By 2005, the lighthouse was surrounded by 20 feet of water from more beach erosion, and the lighthouse toppled into the Gulf of Mexico. While over the years, many unnamed hurricanes not mentioned here have damaged and brought havoc to the southern and gulf area lighthouses, with Hurricanes Helene and Milton in 2024 just being the latest, the lighthouses will still stand and continue to do the job they were built for, even when the weather changes again and its pathways head toward them.

With the erosion of the surrounding land and the continual concerns for weather issues, such as hurricanes and flooding, these lighthouses are constantly subjected to nature's fury. It is the good fortune that many lighthouses are now under the protection of the National Register of Historic Places and that many societies and associations have taken these lighthouses under their protection and continue to keep them safe for future generations to learn about this maritime history.

THE POSTAL ACT. The Postal Act of May 19, 1898, provided for the extensive private product of postcards to measure 3.25 by 5.5 inches. Messages could only be written on the front. The back was reserved "exclusively for the address." After March 1, 1907, the law specified that messages could be written on the backs of cards. Cards of this new style were "divided back" because of the vertical line, to the left of which the message could be written, with the address on the right. Undivided back cards remained in the inventories of shops for many years.

One

Maryland

North Point Range Light, Fort Howard. In 1822, Benjamin Latrobe, a known architect and engineer, designed two whitewashed masonry towers. The lower eastern tower stood in three feet of water, connected to shore by a walkway. The western tower stood in five feet of water, 100 yards from the shore. Both towers had a sixth-order lens. By 1830, the towers needed major work due to poor workmanship when built and were discontinued in 1873.

FENWICK ISLAND LIGHTHOUSE, DELAWARE-MARYLAND STATE LINE. The lighthouse was built on an isolated peninsula in Delaware at the Maryland state line. In 1858, a brick, double-walled, 87-foot tower with a central cast-iron spiral staircase was constructed with a lantern room fitted with a third-order Fresnel lens. The inside diameter at the base of the double-walled tower was 8.5 feet at the base and taper toward the top. A two-story wood-framed keepers' dwelling was also built at the same time just east of the light for both the head keeper and his assistant.

FENWICK ISLAND. In 1878, a second dwelling was built for the head keeper and his family. Because of the dangers around the Fenwick Island Shoal, by 1888, the Fenwick Island Shoal Lightship was anchored to the east of the shoal, within eight miles of the lighthouse itself. The ship anchored there until a lighted buoy was used to replace the ship in 1933. The light was automated in 1978 and soon deactivated, with ownership going to the State of Delaware; with restoration and with the help of a support group, it was rededicated in 1998.

FORT WASHINGTON LIGHTHOUSE, FORT WASHINGTON. Although the fort itself was finished in 1824, it was not until 1856 that a light would be built on the military ground. The original light was an 18.5-foot, cast-iron tower, but its efficiency soon came into question. A new, shorter tower was constructed for more efficiency in 1870, placing the light near the end of a wharf. In 1883, Secretary of War Robert Lincoln gave permission for a "small wood structure suitable for a keepers dwelling" to be built near the tower after several decades of requests. By 1904, the low portion of the tower had been enclosed, making room for supplies to be stored. The light tower was electrified in 1920. (Below, courtesy of the US Coast Guard.)

Turkey Point Lighthouse, Elk Neck State Park, Chesapeake Bay. With the bluffs at 100 feet from the water level, the 35-foot tower was more than tall enough to give it a focal plane of 129 feet when built in 1833. When first built, lamps and reflectors were used until 1855, when a fourth-order Fresnel lens was substituted in the nine-sided lantern room with its pyramidal roof. Where normal iron stairs were quite often used, this lighthouse had wood steps. While originally painted red, the lantern room was repainted in black in the late 1880s. The keepers' house was a one-and-a-half-story brick building, but the need for enlargement came by 1889, and the dwelling had a full second floor added. The light was fully automated in 1947, and the keepers' house was torn down in 1972.

Concord Point Lighthouse, Havre de Grace. The dangerous shoals near the Susquehanna River made a lighthouse a necessity in 1827. A master builder named John Donahoo was responsible for constructing numerous Maryland lighthouses. Soon, Donahoo constructed a 30-foot-tall granite conical tower with spiral granite steps. The walls are 31 inches thick at the base of the light and 18 inches near the top of the tower. Until 1854, whale oil lamps had been used for lighting, and then a sixth-order lens was installed, which was later upgraded to a fifth-order lens.

Concord Point. A four-room, 20-by-34-foot, one-and-a-half-story keepers' house was built out of Port Depot granite, along with an attached kitchen, and constructed across the street from the tower. By 1884, an extra story was added to the keepers' dwelling, adding four rooms and much-needed space. By 1975, Concord Point was decommissioned. A nonprofit group took over the care and maintenance of the tower and the keepers' house. The loss of the original Fresnel lens remains a mystery. The Coast Guard loaned a fifth-order lens for the tower, and it was removed and placed in the museum, housed in the former keepers' dwelling.

Cove Point Lighthouse, Calvert Cliffs Park, Calvert County. In 1828, four acres of land were purchased at Cove Point to mark a shoal that extends far into the shipping channel. A 36-foot-tall, cone-shaped masonry tower was built, along with a one-and-a-half-story keepers' dwelling, 20 by 34 feet, with an attached kitchen made of brick. While the door to the tower faces west, the windows in the tower face north, south, and east. A circular lantern room painted black and stone decking, with safety railing, encircle the top of the tower. With an original fifth-order lens originally used, it would be soon upgraded to a fourth-order lens. By 1883, an extra story was added to the keepers' dwelling to accommodate the extra assistants and their families. In 1925, a dormer was also added for additional space. The lighthouse was automated in 1986.

Cove Point Lighthouse

Cobb Point Bar Lighthouse, Cobb Island. With a narrow and dangerous channel when entering the entrance to the Wicomico River from the Potomac River, a square, screw-pile lighthouse, supported with five iron screw piles, was built in 1889. Housed in the lantern room was a fourth-order Fresnel lens. Damaged by fire in 1939, an automated light was placed on the screw-pile foundation in 1940.

Seven-Foot Knoll Lighthouse, Patapsco River, Baltimore. Built on a rocky shoal, the lighthouse was constructed in 1855 in the Chesapeake Bay. A Baltimore iron foundry fabricated parts of the structure, like walls and beams, and transported them to the site for easy assembly. The light was one story, with a central pile and eight others spaced evenly around the 40-foot diameter iron structure. It had a fourth-order Fresnel lens. The light was automated in 1949.

LAZARETTO POINT LIGHTHOUSE, BALTIMORE. In 1831, at the entrance to the Baltimore Harbor, a light was constructed on Lazaretto Point with a 30-foot tower built with whitewashed bricks. By 1836, a fire would destroy a small hospital near the tower and damage the keepers' house. A new two-story dwelling measuring 20 by 34 feet was constructed of brick and reclaimed materials from the previous dwellings. A fourth-order lens was used by the light after 1855. The area around the point became home to a depot used to resupply other lighthouses in the Chesapeake Bay area. It was also used for the fabrication of screw-pile lighthouses to be towed to their respective needed areas. The tower became electrified in 1914, and then by 1926, the tower was demolished and replaced with a 39-foot steel skeleton tower. (Left, courtesy of Robert Biggy.)

Drum Point Lighthouse, at the Mouth of the Patuxent River. It was not until 1883 that marine traffic warranted the use of the five acres at Drum Point for a light. Wrought-iron piles 10 inches in diameter were used for the foundation, with a white hexagonal cottage-style building, one-and-a-half stories with clapboard siding, and a red metal roof completing the light. The first level was used for living quarters for the keeper, with the second floor carrying a second bedroom and a stairway to the octagonal, black-painted lantern room. The light originally stood in 10 feet of water, but over the years, the land and the sand changed, so that by 1970, the light was on dry land. In 1944, electricity was brought to the light, but it went dark during World War II. With the approach of 1960, the light became semiautomated.

FORT CARROLL LIGHTHOUSE, BALTIMORE HARBOR. The lighthouse was built on a man-made hexagonal island at the mouth of the Patapsco River. As a reaction to the War of 1812, it would still take until 1847 before work on the fort began. The project was supervised by a young Army Corps of Engineers brevet-colonel named Robert E. Lee. The fort was dedicated to the city's resident Charles Carroll, a Maryland politician, who, by that time, was the only surviving signer of the Declaration of Independence. The three-year endeavor was plagued with issues from the very start, from its location in the harbor to the inadequate funds allowed, and Robert E. Lee had left by 1852 to become a superintendent of West Point. A light with a sixth-order Fresnel lens was added to the keepers' dwelling by 1854.

FORT CARROLL. The fort was only partially completed at the time of the Civil War and was very nearly considered obsolete by that time. The light was removed by 1875 because of the instability of the keepers' dwelling. A new two-story keepers' house was built in 1888 to house the light once again. Over the next 20-some years, the light was moved around to different parts of the island. By the time of World War I, the light was an important part of Baltimore's submarine defense system. By 1900, the casement around the light tower was demolished, and now the lower area is open, leaving the structure as it is seen today, sitting on the fortress walls. By 1958, the light and island were sold into private hands.

Located on a peninsula in the harbor of historic and picturesque St. Michaels, the Chesapeake Bay Maritime Museum has grown from a single house when established in 1965 to a 16-acre complex of restored buildings and new structures erected to exhibit a comprehensive collection of Bay artifacts and to preserve the lore of the area.

Exhibits at the Museum trace the history of the Bay and its traditions in boat building, commercial fishing, yachting, waterfowling and navigation. Major features include a 100-year-old "screwpile" lighthouse, a restored log-bottom bugeye, a skipjack, a racing log canoe, an important collection of Bay small craft types, a comprehensive decoy and waterfowling presentation, the Howard I. Chapelle Memorial Library, which is a valuable source for scholars and students of the Chesapeake, and other attractions.

HOOPER STRAIT LIGHTHOUSE, BLOODSWORTH ISLAND, CHESAPEAKE BAY. The screw-pile lighthouse was built in Hooper Strait in 1867 as a square dwelling with a lantern room on the roof that housed the fifth-order lens. By 1877, during an ice storm, the foundation braces gave way, and the dwelling sank up to its roofline. In 1878, a new hexagon-shaped white cottage-style screw-pile structure was placed back in Hooper Strait. The year 1954 saw the lighthouse become automated. By 1966, the Chesapeake Bay Maritime Museum stepped in and stopped the destruction of the lighthouse after the Coast Guard deemed it ready for demolition. The light was moved by barge 40 miles to St. Michael's on Navy Point, where a new steel foundation was waiting for it. Since 2004, Hooper Strait Lighthouse has been giving visitors the screw-pile lighthouse experience.

Two

Virginia

Old Point Comfort Lighthouse, Hampton Roads. At the entrance to Hampton Roads is where, in 1803, at Fort George, a 54-foot octagonal stone tower with a spiral staircase of hand-cut stone that leads to the lantern room was built. The United States lost control of the light during the War of 1812 after it fell into the hands of the British.

FORT MONROE LIGHTHOUSE. After the war, Robert E. Lee, a lieutenant of engineers, helped transform the area and spent three years helping to complete the construction of Fort Monroe, the largest stone fort constructed in the United States. While Congress urged that the lighthouse be moved into the fort area, the move was never made, and the light sits outside the fort area today. The lighthouse managed to evade any destruction that might have been caused by the Civil War and remained in Union hands throughout. The lighthouse hosted President Lincoln in 1862 to survey the troops. A new keepers' house was constructed in the Queen Anne style in 1891 to replace the original dwelling. The light has been preserved due to the diligence of the National Park Service and the Fort Monroe Authority.

New Point Comfort Lighthouse, Chesapeake Bay. New Point Comfort Lighthouse was constructed in 1804 on a small three-fourths of a mile-long island along a narrow passage called Deep Creek that separated it from the mainland. An octagonal 63-foot sandstone tower was constructed with an attached two-story brick dwelling. By 1865, the tower had a fourth-order Fresnel lens, with a visibility of 13 miles, while the dwelling and outbuildings still stood on firm ground. By 1928, the keepers' dwelling is gone, and the water is encroaching near the tower. A hurricane in 1933 separated the tower from the rest of the island by a channel. In 1950, the lighthouse would be converted to electricity, but by 1963, it would become decommissioned. Restoration and support have been carried out by the Mathews County Historical Society.

LIGHTHOUSE ON NEW POINT BEACH, MATHEWS COUNTY, VA

Assateague Lighthouse, Chincoteague. After issues with the first 1833 lighthouse, in 1865, after the Civil War, work started up on a bluff for the 140-foot, conical, redbrick tower. A bridge had been built in 1862 between Assateague Island and Chincoteague, the nearest town, helping pave the way for this newer lighthouse tower. In 1868, the tower would receive its distinctive red and white bands for its daymark. The foundation that the tower and the one-story entrance were constructed on has a 12-foot-deep stone and concrete base. Because of the height, four windows face north, and three windows face south to give light to the interior of the tower. A keepers' dwelling was finished at the same time as the tower using a duplex construction for both head and assistant keepers.

ASSATEAGUE LIGHT. In 1893, a major remodeling took place to make more comfortable lodgings for the keepers and their families, and the larger dwelling became known as the "Keepers Mansion." It had three apartments with a living area, kitchen, dining room, bathroom, and three bedrooms each. In 1900, the area surrounding the tower was graded flat with a marsh sod layer to help with the sand and erosion. In 1933, electricity came to the tower, and three 100-watt bulbs were used inside the Fresnel lens. With a clock turning the light on and off at the prescribed times, it made an on-site keeper unnecessary, and soon, the keepers' dwelling was sold. In 2004, the lighthouse was transferred from the US Coast Guard to the US Fish and Wildlife Service.

WINDMILL POINT LIGHTHOUSE, MOUTH OF THE RAPPAHANNOCK RIVER. Lightships in the past had lit the Rappahannock Spit shoal, but during the Civil War, the Confederate soldiers extinguished the light, removing that protection. In 1869, a screw-pile-style light was placed next to the shoal. The iron screw piles were penetrated to six feet. The iron was painted red, with the structure painted a straw color. The year 1954 saw the light come under automatic operation. The light was sold into private ownership in 1967 and removed.

DEEP WATER SHOALS, THE JAMES RIVER. The screw-pile-style lighthouse was first lit in 1855 with a 20-foot square foundation on five-foot diameter iron screw piles. The dwelling was a 20-foot square, with an internal ladder leading to a lantern room. The light was damaged in 1867 with ice damage to the pilings. In 1868, a new screw-pile-style lighthouse was built, with this light being torn down in 1966.

Stingray Point Lighthouse, Deltaville. In the early 1600s, an English adventurer, while spearfishing, was stung by a stingray, and from then on, the tip of the peninsula on the southern side of the Rappahannock River was known as Stingray Point. A wooden hexagonal lighthouse built in the screw-pile style, with three rooms and a center-mounted lantern room, had a sixth-order Fresnel lens that lit the peninsula in 1859.

Thimble Shoal Lighthouse, Chesapeake Bay. The screw-pile hexagon lighthouse was constructed in 1872, then destroyed in a fire in 1880, making necessary the construction of a new keepers' quarters. There were numerous ship collisions, but the last one was in 1909, when a new caisson-style light filled with concrete and standing 55 feet above the bay was built. It housed a fourth-order Fresnel lens. The cylindrical tower would have portholes for light. It was not until the 2000s that the skeleton remains of the old screw pile was removed.

Jones Point Lighthouse, Alexandria. Dangerous sandbars along the Potomac River between Georgetown, Alexandria, and Washington City necessitated a lighthouse at Jones Point. When constructed and finished, the light was first lit in 1856, with a brick foundation as the base and a rectangular, clapboard Greek Revival–style dwelling with a round lantern room on the pitched roofline. There were two large rooms with fireplaces and a full basement, along with a dormer room in the attic, where a ladder provided access to the lantern room. The lighthouse dwelling was originally painted white with a black lantern room. In 1900, the lens had a solid red characteristic light, which caused some confusion within the area, and by 1919, its characteristics changed to a flashing white light. The light was decommissioned in 1962.

Jordan Point Lighthouse, South Bank of the Jordan River. In 1855, a keepers' dwelling with a masthead light on the roof saw a replacement by 1875 of a self-standing pyramidal 35-foot wooden tower housing a sixth-order Fresnel lens. The lightkeepers would have a new and larger dwelling in 1888. With the light station's deactivation in 1927, the wooden lighthouse tower was demolished, and a steel skeleton tower replaced it. The keepers' house was sold into private hands and is now a residence. (Below, courtesy of the US Coast Guard.)

OLD POINT HENRY LIGHTHOUSE, VIRGINIA BEACH. It was Old Cape Henry that was the first lighthouse fully authorized by the new United States and the First Congress in 1792. Cape Henry sits between the Atlantic Ocean and the Chesapeake Bay, with Washington, DC; Baltimore; Norfolk; and Newport News as ports of entry. The light was in the process of construction when the Revolutionary War intervened, and it was after the war that the funds were reestablished for the finishing of the project. An octagonal, 90-foot-tall, eight-sided pyramid tower was made of sandstone. At the same time, a 20-foot-square, two-story dwelling was constructed for the living quarters of the keeper. Repairs and upgrades were necessary for the coming years, with a new keepers' dwelling built in 1835. The light went on to be declared a National Historic Landmark in 1964.

New Point Henry Lighthouse, Virginia Beach. By 1872, structural damage was found to be overtaking the Old Point Henry Light, and a replacement needed to be built. A 157-foot tower made of cast and wrought iron housed a first-order Fresnel lens in the lantern room. The new light stands only 350 feet from the old tower. The daymark given to this new light has very distinctive coloring. The octagonal tower has alternating white and black colors on the various sides, with the colors changing halfway up, giving the tower a checkerboard look about it. Many upgrades were done at the light over the years, including a radio beacon in 1923 and a fog signal testing laboratory in 1934. The light became fully automated in 1983 and is still in use today. The old tower still stands as a daymark with use for triangulation.

Cape Charles Lighthouse, Smith Island. Cape Charles has the distinction of being the tallest light tower in Virginia. This cast-iron, pyramidal, skeleton, white tower is the third light to be placed in the same general location. The first light tower was a 55-foot concrete tower built in 1828. By 1864, a second concrete 150-foot tower was built very near to the first light. With erosion, a constant source of problems, this third tower, at 191 feet, was constructed in 1895, with a central iron circular tower, eight iron legs surrounding that center tube, and a first-order Fresnel lens. The light became fully automated in 1963. The light was decommissioned by the US Coast Guard in 2019. (Above, courtesy of the US Coast Guard.)

Three

North Carolina

The Tallest Lighthouse in the United States. North Carolina is home to a group of barrier islands that separate the Atlantic Ocean and the river inlets called the Outer Banks. Hatteras Island is where the first lighthouse, a 90-foot-high sandstone tower, was first lit in 1803. By 1853, the inadequacy of the original height made it necessary to bring the height to 208 feet and add a first-order Fresnel lens to the lantern room. The daymark had the lower portion painted gray with the upper portion red.

CAPE HATTERAS LIGHTHOUSE, HATTERAS ISLAND, BUXTON. After the Civil War and the destruction that accorded the lighthouse, a new 198-foot-tall, brick conical-shaped tower was constructed in 1870. It was given a black-and-white daymark in a distinctive barber pole paint job with a redbrick and granite foundation. This light also was given a first-order Fresnel lens with a visibility of 20 miles. A 268-foot climb will get one to the top of the light tower. The old tower was demolished in 1871, and it would take until 1980 for those ruins to be finally washed away. Almost from the start, there was concern because of the sand erosion that continued to occur throughout the years. By 1999, the tower was just 15 feet from the water's edge; the lighthouse was then moved 2,900 feet away from the erosion of the shoreline at a cost of $12 million.

Currituck Beach Lighthouse, Corolla. The Currituck Beach Lighthouse was the northernmost light in the Outer Banks of North Carolina when constructed in 1875. The 162-foot-tall, brick conical tower was constructed with an octagonal stone base. The lantern room housed a first-order Fresnel lens with a visibility of 21 miles. While almost every other lighthouse had daymarks painted on the brick, the Currituck Lighthouse retained the original natural brick covering. Three keepers—a head and two assistants—and their families shared the Victorian duplex constructed for their use. In 1900, Orville and Wilber Wright, two bicycle shop owners, while working on their "flying machine" at Kill Devil Hills, became fast friends with the keeper of the light, William Tate. The light became automated in 1939. After World War II, the property was abandoned, and the tower fell into disrepair. Now, the light tower is in the hands of the Outer Banks Conservationists.

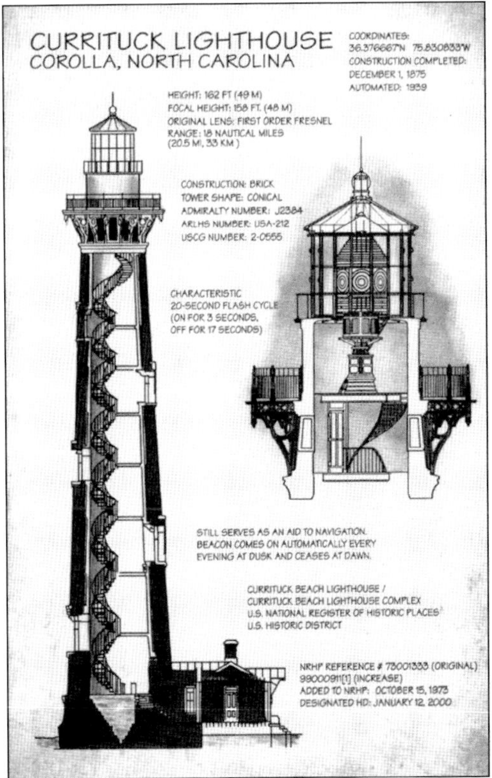

Cape Lookout Lighthouse, Carteret County. The first lighthouse at Cape Lookout was a 96-foot tower constructed of brick and wood, with red-and-white-painted diagonal stripes with wood shingles. The light was never tall enough, and by 1859, a new 163-foot brick tower was constructed and used the first-order Fresnel lens from the previous light, giving the tower a visibility of over 19 miles. As with a lot of the lighthouses in the Outer Banks, the Civil War would have a devastating effect on the light. After the war, very quickly, damages to the Fresnel lens and the iron stairway were repaired. The year 1873 saw a new keepers' quarters constructed, large enough for a head keeper and two assistants. A second head keepers' dwelling was built in 1907 to ease the cramped quarters of the families stationed there.

THE DIAMOND LADY LIGHTHOUSE. In 1873, the lighthouse took on its distinctive daymark with large painted diagonal and alternating black-and-white diamonds, with thoughts that the black diamonds are facing north and south and the white diamonds are facing east and west. The light would see itself through World War II as a lookout for enemy submarines. The light was automated in 1950. The erosion from the tidal currents along the beach became a great concern for the safety of the light tower. Friends of Cape Lookout National Seashore was formed in 2008 to help with repair work and making the structure safe, with the intent of allowing climbing to continue at the tower.

Bodie Island Lighthouse, North Nags Head. This Bodie Island Lighthouse is the third attempt to light the portion of the peninsula on the Roanoke Sound side of what is now known as the Cape Hatteras National Seashore. The first lighthouse was built in 1847, but foundation conditions would make it necessary for a new light to be constructed in 1859. The second lighthouse was destroyed during the Civil War in 1861, when the tower was packed with explosives. In 1872, a mile and a half north and farther inland from the former location, the octagonal granite block foundation was laid for the 164-foot tower painted with black-and-white horizontal stripes. A spiral staircase led to the lantern room housing a first-order Fresnel lens, offering a visibility of 18 miles.

ADDITIONAL BODIE ISLAND VIEWS. A keepers' dwelling was constructed just to the west of the tower, which provided room to house the head keeper and his assistant. Unfortunately, there was not enough room for them to bring their families along with them. Money was then appropriated to fix the situation, but with the high construction costs and the isolated area, it became more beneficial to eliminate the second assistant keeper position. In the late 1920s and early 1930s, with a bridge constructed to connect to the island, the isolation was reduced somewhat for the families living there. The lighthouse was fully automated in 1940 after the US Coast Guard took control of the light in 1939. The National Park Service took control of the lighthouse in 2000.

OCRACOKE LIGHTHOUSE, OCRACOKE ISLAND. Built on relatively higher ground in 1823 with a foundation of stone and timber, the 76-foot conical tower was constructed of brick with a mortar surface. The mortar, constructed out of a combination of lime, ground rice, clear glue, and salt and mixed with boiling water, was applied to the bricks while hot. In 1849, a new lantern room was added, and 1854 saw a fourth-order Fresnel lens added to replace the brass lamps previously used. Surviving the Civil War with minimal damage, the only need was to reassemble the dismantled lens. By 1900, the light was electrified, giving it a visibility of 14 miles. Its daymark has always been that of a white tower.

ADDITIONAL VIEWS OF OCRACOKE LIGHTHOUSE. The original keepers' dwelling was a one-story building with three rooms. The year 1897 saw the roof removed and a second story attached with an additional three rooms. The keepers' dwelling saw an addition in 1929, creating a duplex situation. The original wooden spiral steps had been built on the outside of the light on the exterior wall in 1950; they were removed due to the rotting wood, and a steel spiral staircase used for maintenance and access was constructed inside the tower. In 2010, the first work was completed on the light since the US Coast Guard turned the light over to the National Park Service with new glass in the lantern room and the metalwork repaired.

Roanoke River Light, Albemarle Sound. The first structure was built in 1866 as a square, screw-pile lighthouse in Albemarle Sound at the mouth of the Roanoke River. In 1885, the lighthouse was rebuilt after a fire, but within the same year, an ice storm damaged the pilings, making the need to again rebuild in 1887. This lighthouse was also a screw-pile style with two stories and a lantern room with a fourth-order Fresnel lens in a tower rising from the corner of the building. The light was decommissioned in 1941. In 2010, restoration efforts were started.

Diamond Shoals Lighthouse, Dare County. The Outer Banks is a group of barrier islands 25 miles out into the Atlantic Ocean, with Diamond Shoals a farther seven miles away, where only a narrow band of water between the Gulf Stream and Diamond Shoals made passage safe for mariners. Lightships were used at Diamond Shoals for many years until a permanent structure was built in 1966, with full automation in 1977. The light was extinguished in 2001.

Bald Head Lighthouse, Bald Head Island. The first lighthouse was built along the Cape Fear River in 1792. The replacement lighthouse built farther inland would be known as "Old Baldy" in 1817. The octagonal brick tower reached a height of 110 feet, had a layer of stucco added to the bricks, and was given a coat of white paint. Originally equipped with lamps and reflectors, it was not until 1855 that a third-order Fresnel lens was put into use. Because of the location being four miles from the coast and the lack of height for the tower, in 1898, the building of a new 184-foot, cast-iron skeleton tower housing a first-order Fresnel lens was found to be of better use to the maritime traffic near the shoals. Old Baldy continued to serve alongside the new Cape Fear Lighthouse until 1935. (Above, courtesy of the National Archives.)

PRICES CREEK LIGHT, SOUTHPORT, N. C.

PRICE'S CREEK LIGHTHOUSE, SOUTHPORT. Prices's Creek Lighthouse, when used as a part of a set of range lights, was the shorter of the lights placed in front of a taller light, showing the mariners that if lined up together, the ships would be in the center of the harbor or channel. Constructed entirely of brick in 1849, the front range tower called Price's Creek was 20 feet tall. A second range light, located 800 feet away, was a large square brick structure that served as the keepers' dwelling as well. The range lights would serve to guide Confederate blockade runners past the Union ships just offshore during the Civil War. The rear range lighthouse was damaged in a storm and soon torn down, making the front range obsolete. It soon went into disrepair.

Four

SOUTH CAROLINA

BULLS BAY LIGHTHOUSE, CHARLESTON COUNTY. The original Bulls Bay lighthouse was built in 1854. Completed was a one-and-a-half-story keepers' dwelling with a tower and lantern room on the front of the roofline, similar to many lighthouses on the Pacific coast. During the Civil War, the Confederates built an encampment very near to the light and then proceeded to damage the lens and lantern to keep it out of Union control. The Union forces destroyed the encampment, but not before the keepers' house was set on fire. After the war, the light was relit, but by 1897, erosion would wash the dwelling and tower away. (Courtesy of the National Archives.)

Morris Island Lighthouse, Morris Island, Charleston Harbor. King George III ordered the construction of a lighthouse on the south side to the entrance of Charleston Harbor in 1767. The tower eventually reached 161 feet after its rebuilding through the Civil War years and after, when it was then listed as the tallest lighthouse in South Carolina. Morris Island had enough room for the light to be located roughly 1,200 feet from the shoreline. Over time and after the construction of the jetty in Charleston Harbor, the currents changed, and the erosion of the island began very quickly. By 1938, the lighthouse became automated, and a keeper was no longer needed, with the shoreline now reaching the tower foundation. The Morris Island Light was decommissioned in 1962.

Hunting Island Lighthouse, Hunting Island, Beaufort. The first Hunting Island Light was blown up in 1861 by a retreating Confederate army to hinder the advancing Union army. Eight-foot-thick concrete was used as a foundation for the new lighthouse in 1874. The tower, constructed with a metal shell and brick, had a height of 121 feet, and the lantern room housed a second-order Fresnel lens. The head keeper and his two assistants had a spacious 12-room, two-and-a-half-story dwelling by 1876. The lighthouse felt the effects of an earthquake but suffered no lasting damage in 1886. The area where the light stood experienced rapid erosion by 1899, and it needed to be moved. The light was dismantled and moved by way of a tramway and then reassembled approximately one-and-a-quarter mile farther inland. The lighthouse was deactivated in 1933.

FORT SUMTER RANGE LIGHTHOUSE, CHARLESTON HARBOR. Fort Sumter was built in 1829 on a sandbar at the entrance to Charleston Harbor, where work on the fort would take until the start of the Civil War in 1861 to finish. An octagonal-shaped brick tower was built on the top of one of the circular stairways in 1856 and used a fifth-order Fresnel lens. The Union forces pulled out when the Confederate artillery battered the fort, and South Carolina became the first state to secede from the Union. Between the Union and Confederate forces, the fort and lighthouse would sustain numerous damages throughout the war.

Fort Sumter. In 1872, the light tower was relocated to the east side of the fort during the rebuilding process. Ten years later, it was moved to the northwest side of the fort. In 1886, Fort Sumter would feel the effects of an earthquake over a number of weeks. By 1893, the front light was destroyed in a hurricane when the storm surge flooded the fort and washed away the keepers' dwelling, along with other significant damages. The new tower, while erected to replace the damaged tower, now had a green metal skeletal tower as the front range light, and the rear range light would be located at St. Philip's Church steeple until 1915. The front range light was decommissioned in 1950.

GEORGETOWN LIGHTHOUSE, WINYAH BAY. Ships enter Winyah Bay by passing between the North and South Islands, and the Georgetown Lighthouse was built on North Island in 1801 when John Adams was still president. The 72-foot pyramidal wood tower and two-story keepers' dwelling would only last until 1806 due to storm damage. By 1811, a brick lighthouse with a stone stairway was constructed. During the Civil War, the tower was used as a lookout post and was heavily damaged during that conflict. After the war, the tower was heightened to 87 feet, and a two-story keepers' dwelling was added to the station. The North Island, where the Georgetown Light was situated, managed to evade any damage in the Charleston earthquake in 1886. The Georgetown Light is the oldest lighthouse in South Carolina and became automated in 1986.

Cape Romain Lighthouse, Charleston County. Normally, when a new lighthouse is built, the old one is torn down and debris is removed. In the case of Cape Romain, when the old light, a 65-foot tower with reflectors, became inefficient, it was kept. Located on Lighthouse Island, in 1854, a 150-foot tower with a first-order Fresnel lens was constructed to ease the shipping through the dangerous shoals. This light also saw conflict in the Civil War. After the war, with its foundation settling, the light soon had a three-foot tilt toward the mainland. Along with the new light, three new keepers' dwellings were constructed. The tower's daymark had a white lower half, and the eight sides of the upper portion were painted alternately white and black. The old light was painted red. The light was discontinued in 1947.

HILTON HEAD ISLAND REAR RANGE LIGHTHOUSE, HILTON HEAD ISLAND. This rear range light was constructed in 1879 as a cast-iron, 87-foot skeleton tower on six concrete piers. A cylindrical center stair tower has a spiral staircase leading to the hexagonal wooden lantern room. The station was deactivated in 1932.

DAUFUSKIE ISLAND (HAIG POINT) REAR RANGE LIGHTHOUSE, BEAUFORT COUNTY. On the northeast end of Daufuskie Island is the Calibogue Sound, where a set of range lights was constructed in 1873. The rear range lighthouse was constructed as a white-painted, wooden, two-story Victorian dwelling, with a square tower extending from the eastern end of the pitched roofline. A fifth-order Fresnel lens was housed in the lantern room. The light was deactivated in 1924.

Five

Georgia

Tybee Island Lighthouse, Tybee Island. Located at the northeast end of Tybee Island, next to the Savannah River, the original 90-foot wooden tower was built in 1736. After a storm damaged it beyond repair, a new stone tower was its replacement in 1741. That tower was lost to the erosion of the sea, and in 1773, a brick tower, 100 feet tall and built farther inland from the shore, lit the Savannah River shipping lanes.

TYBEE ISLAND. In 1822, a 50-foot tower was built on the seaward side of a 100-foot tower and, using lamps in the shorter tower paired with the main tower, made it function as a set of range lights. The Tybee Light was given a second-order lens, while the front light was given a fourth-order lens. The Confederate forces abandoned the light during the Civil War, setting fire to the wooden stairs and landings. Only the bottom 60 feet were salvageable. After the war, plans were made to make the tower a total of 154 feet with a cast-iron spiral staircase; it had a painted-white daymark when finished. Cracks emerged after a hurricane in 1871, followed by an earthquake in 1886, with repair work being needed to shore up the tower once again. The daymark on the tower would change numerous times until it had a black-white-black daymark.

Sapelo Island Light, Darien. When built in 1820, the Sapelo Island Lighthouse became another of the many Winslow Lewis lighthouses among the Southern Atlantic lights. Located on the southern tip of the island, it was a guide for maritime shipping for getting through the Doby Sound to the Port of Darien. The lighthouse was a 65-foot brick structure with thick brick walls. It used lamps and reflectors when first built, and then in the 1850s, the tower was raised an additional 10 feet, and a fourth-order Fresnel lens was housed in the lantern room. After the Civil War, extensive repairs were needed, with a new keepers' dwelling and a new lantern room to allow the lens to be put back after it had been removed during the war. Following an 1898 storm, a new skeleton-style light was constructed. By the 1930s, both lights could still be seen, with the brick light having its three large stripes of red prominently shown.

St. Simons Island Lighthouse, St. Simons Island. A 75-foot octagonal tower in the Early Federal style was built on the island in 1810. In 1856, the lamps and reflectors originally used in the lantern room were removed and then outfitted with a third-order Fresnel lens. In 1862, when the Confederates fled the island during the Civil War, they used dynamite to try and destroy the keepers' house and tower to cause obstruction to the Union forces. A new light was constructed after the war to a height of 104 feet, as was a lantern room housing a third-order lens and a Victorian duplex for the keepers to reside.

ST. SIMONS ISLAND LIGHT. By 1880, not all was smooth going for the residents at St. Simons when a duel was to take place between two keepers; a death occurred, stemming from accounts of unwanted advances and inappropriate remarks made to their wives. In 1893, funds were approved through Congress to set another light on the island to use as a range light in the form of a skeleton tower, which was promptly demolished in a hurricane and replaced shortly after. Electricity came to the light station in 1934, and 16 years later, in 1950, the light was automated. The Coastal Georgia Historical Society took the transfer of the station in 2004.

Cockspur Island Lighthouse, Chatham County. In 1849, two lights were built to show the entrance to the south channel of the Savannah River, and one was called Cockspur Island Lighthouse. In 1854, a hurricane damaged the tower and keepers' house, making it necessary to rebuild a brick tower with a design on its eastern side in the shape of the prow of a ship to combat the high seas. Considering fighting through the Civil War went on around the lighthouse, it never incurred any damage. In 1909, because of the changing currents and the now deeper water of the North Channel, the lighthouse was found to be unnecessary and was soon deactivated. A restoration effort helped preserve the tower with a new lantern room with the help of the Tybee Historical Society and Friends of the Cockspur Island Lighthouse. (Above, courtesy of the National Archives.)

LITTLE CUMBERLAND ISLAND LIGHTHOUSE, ST. ANDREW SOUND. Cumberland Island is the largest and longest island and the southernmost one along the barrier islands stretching from Florida to South Carolina. A 60-foot circular brick tower with a third-order lens built in 1838, along with a keepers' house and a warehouse, made up the small light station. Although it survived the Civil War, extensive damage occurred, requiring repairs. Along with erosion on the coast, a needed brick wall was built to protect the tower where, over the years, the sand dunes made almost invisible. The light was decommissioned in 1915. The Little Cumberland Island Association purchased the lighthouse in 1961. Restoration efforts took effect, and unsafe, unused buildings were removed from the site. (Both, courtesy of the US Coast Guard.)

Tybee Knoll Cut Range Lighthouse, Savannah River. A lightship was first used in the area before the light station was constructed and took the place of the vessel starting in 1870, when work began. By 1874, a square screw-pile lighthouse built on five wooden piles encased in cast iron, with a fifth-order lens in the lantern room, was finished. Because of the need for a set of range lights to be effective in the area, the lightship remained until 1880, when the beacons were in place. By 1886, a long plank walkway was built, and piles were driven into the ground for the wharf. In 1919, the tower was raised 16 feet on the dwelling and became the rear range light with the construction of a front range light on a pipe tower. (Courtesy of the US Coast Guard.)

Six

Florida

Amelia Island Lighthouse, Fernandina Beach. The lighthouse is located in the northeastern part of the state, at the north end of Amelia Island, which is part of the northernmost barrier islands on Florida's Atlantic coast. Not far from Jacksonville, this lighthouse is known as the oldest existing lighthouse in the state of Florida; it lights the entrance to Fernandina Beach Harbor, Georgia's Cumberland Sound, and St. Mary's River, where it empties into the Atlantic Ocean.

FERNANDINA BEACH LIGHTHOUSE. A lighthouse was built on Cumberland Island in 1820 because it was the southernmost site in the United States along the Atlantic coast. When Spain ceded Florida to the United States in 1821, and with changes made to the channel, the light on Cumberland Island could no longer be seen by maritime traffic. In 1838, the Cumberland Island Light, with its 50-foot tower, was carefully dismantled one brick at a time. The materials were then taken across the river and reconstructed on the highest area on Amelia Island. Range lights were used at various times in the form of beacon lights.

Fernandina Beach. In 1856, the tower was upgraded to a third-order Fresnel lens, letting go of the lamps and reflectors used at the time. With the tower being shut down during the Civil War, it was quickly returned to service, having been spared little damage. In 1871, range light beacons were put into use and displayed in a short square tower mounted on the roof of a two-and-a-half-story keepers' dwelling. In 1881, the tower was raised to 64 feet when a new and larger lantern room was added that would better fit the third-order lens in use. The station became automated in 1970 and with it came the retirement of the last Coast Guard keeper.

THE LIGHTHOUSE FERNANDINA, FLORIDA

Key West Lighthouse, Whiteheads Point. The first 65-foot brick tower built in 1826 used 15 lamps and reflectors and was fueled by whale oil for the light source. In 1846, a major hurricane bore down on the point of Key West, and with a five-foot storm surge, the island was severely damaged, and many lives were lost when the tower collapsed into the sea. A new 50-foot conical tower was placed farther inland on a rise of land in 1848. The US Lighthouse Board started using Fresnel lenses during the mid-1850s, and Key West saw a third-order Fresnel lens housed in its lantern room by 1858. The first of two moves to give extra height to the tower started in 1872 when five feet were added along with a new lantern room.

Key West. With the growth of both the town and the mature trees in the area, the need to add extra height to the tower would take place in 1894. The tower was then raised 20 feet higher and again used the third-order lens of the original light. A new keepers' quarters was added to the station in 1887 for the keeper, his assistant, and their families. The tower survived numerous storms and hurricanes over the coming years, but by 1915, the necessity for a light keeper was dispensed with. While the US Coast Guard took over ownership of the light in 1939, by 1966 the Key West Art and Historical Society was given control, and 1969 brought a final deactivation. Restoration took place, and soon, the station was opened as a museum.

Cape Florida Lighthouse, Key Biscayne. The lighthouse placed at the south end of Key Biscayne on the Atlantic side was used to help mariners avoid the reef that extends from the Key Biscayne area to the Florida Keys. The original light, built in 1825, was a 65-foot brick tower, but with an Indian attack and a fire that burned the wood stairs and damaged the tower, it was not until 1847 before it could be rebuilt—this time with iron stairs. The tower gained added height in 1855, to a total of 95 feet, and housed a second-order Fresnel lens in the lantern room, all on the recommendations of Lt. George G. Meade, who later went on to be commander of the Army of the Potomac.

Cape Florida. In 1861, when Florida seceded from the Union, the light went dark when the lamp was removed, and the prisms were damaged in an effort to see that they would not be used to help the Union sailors in the area. By 1866, the light was repaired and put back into service. In 1878, the light was once again extinguished when the Fowey Rocks Lighthouse was built to replace it. By the 1920s, the erosion around the tower had brought the water only 10 feet from the tower itself. The State of Florida purchased the tower in 1966 to become part of a state park. Hurricane Andrew created damage that necessitated major repairs. The light tower is now used as a private aid to navigation.

JUPITER INLET LIGHTHOUSE, JUPITER. With dangerous shoals near the Jupiter Inlet, the need for a lighthouse on the north side of the inlet was determined in 1853. Lt. George Meade, then an engineer, submitted a design for the building of the lighthouse. By 1860, the brick conical-shaped tower was constructed to a height of 108 feet, with a lantern room housing the first-order Fresnel lens with a 24-mile visibility out to sea. A head keeper and two assistants lived in the two-story dwelling built near the tower. In 1861, vandals removed the lighting apparatus, and the tower remained dark until after the Civil War. The tower was painted red in 1910 because of the discoloration caused by the humidity. The Loxahatchee River Historical Society was founded in 1972 to help preserve the integrity of the tower.

CAPE CANAVERAL LIGHTHOUSE, CAPE CANAVERAL. At approximately one mile inland from shore, the second lighthouse at Cape Canaveral was started in 1859. Work stopped on this tower during the Civil War and resumed again in 1867. The 151-foot tower was built of metal plates with a brick lining and a lantern room housing a first-order-Fresnel lens. The lower three levels were used as living space for the keepers, with a kitchen, living room, and bedrooms. An exterior stairway was added for use by the head keeper, who had a dwelling outside the tower. Originally painted white, by 1873, the distinctive black-and-white bands became the new daymark. By 1883, a new head keepers' dwelling was built, and the previous dwelling was used for the assistants, who found living in a metal tower unbearable during the summer heat. The light was automated in 1967. (Above, courtesy of US Coast Guard.)

St. Augustine Lighthouse, Anastasia Island. An old Spanish tower was converted into a 30-foot lighthouse in 1823 after the United States took control of the Florida Territory. With an increase in height to 50 feet and the addition of a fourth-order Fresnel lens in 1854, that light burned until the lens was removed at the start of the Civil War. Relit after the war but erosion being a concern, a new lighthouse more than one-half-mile inland was soon considered. By 1874, the new brick tower was working with a fixed white light with a focal length of 165 feet. A small brick building attached to the base of the tower was used as a keepers' office and storage building. The tower was painted in black-and-white swirling bands, very similar to Cape Hatteras.

St. Augustine. With the construction of the new tower in progress, it became apparent that the site would need at least three keepers, a head and two assistants. Housing these workers and their families needed to be addressed, and a new dwelling was finished in 1875. The dwelling was made as a duplex, with the head keeper on one side and the first assistant keeper on the other side, leaving the second keeper with a couple of small rooms on the upper floor space. In 1880, the original tower fell over into the sea. In 1888, outside kitchens were built of brick and attached to each end of the structure. Electricity was brought to the tower in 1936, which lessened the keepers' responsibilities. By 1971, the light had become fully automated.

Hillsboro Inlet Lighthouse, Hillsboro Beach. The hazardous area around Hillsboro Point made lighting the area a necessary option for the US government, where the northernmost limit of the Florida Reef, a coral formation, resides. It would take a number of years and requests before the light was established in 1907 when a 137-foot octagonal skeleton tower with a second-order Fresnel lens was constructed. Along with the tower, three keepers' dwellings and work buildings were added to the light station. The lighthouse station saw the effects of the hurricanes of 1926 and 1936. By 1947, another hurricane destroyed the keepers' dwellings.

Hillsboro Light House adjoins Hillsboro Club
Pompano, Florida

Hillsboro Inlet. In 1932, the light station received electricity and full automation by 1974. The Hillsboro Lighthouse Preservation Society was created to help reactivate the Fresnel lens after the lens failure in 1992. In 2003, the US Postal Service issued a set of stamps featuring southeastern lighthouses, and the Hillsboro Inlet was selected to represent the state of Florida. Between 1885 and 1892, postal letter carriers traveled the 68-mile-long coastline between Palm Beach and Miami, with 28 miles by small boat and the remaining 40 miles spent walking along the sand at the water's edge. The waterway was crossed by a rowboat kept at the Hillsboro Inlet for that purpose.

PONCE DE LEON INLET LIGHTHOUSE, PONCE INLET. The first light built was a 45-foot brick conical tower in 1835, where shortly after it was finished, a storm washed away the foundation, and along with the Second Seminole War, the tower's fate was sealed. With the repair work unable to be finished due to the troubled relations with the area's Native Americans, the tower collapsed into the sea in 1836. It was not until after the Civil War that Congress took up the requests for a new light at Mosquito Inlet. The tallest lighthouse in Florida sits at a point between the Halifax River on the north and the Indian River on the south, and its location is the Mosquito Inlet, now known as the Ponce de Leon Inlet.

PONCE DE LEON INLET. Built on the north side of the inlet in 1887, the new 175-foot brick tower had a brick foundation extending 12 feet below the ground to support it. This light served as both a coastal and harbor light because it was placed roughly halfway between the St. Augustine Light and Cape Canaveral Light. A circular 194-step stairway is used to get to the lantern room, housing a first-order Fresnel lens. Separate dwellings were then built to house the head keeper and his assistants at a convenient distance from the tower. In 1926, the Mosquito Inlet became Ponce de Leon Inlet, named after the explorer, because the original name seemed to put off new settlers to the area. Electrified in 1933, the light was fully automated in 1953.

FOWEY ROCKS LIGHTHOUSE, SOUTHEAST OF CAPE FLORIDA. In 1878, the Fowey Rocks Lighthouse was built seven miles southwest of the Cape Florida Lighthouse it would replace. The cast-iron, screw-pile-style light was constructed with a screw pile foundation, a platform building, and a skeletal tower. The lantern room housed a first-order Fresnel lens, with the tower at a height of 110 feet above the water. The light was named after the Royal Navy frigate HMS *Fowey*, which floundered on the reef in 1748; the reef also went on to carry the name.

Sand Key Lighthouse, Southwest of Key West. Located almost seven miles from Key West, the Sand Key Lighthouse is situated next to a channel that leads to Key West, where the submerged reefs and sand created a small island. After the first tower was swept away during a hurricane in 1846, this second light tower was completed in 1853, with a screw-pile foundation and open framework tower, which allowed for the lighthouse to survive the many storms and hurricanes that came to the area. Over the years, each hurricane that hit would take out more of the sand island.

SANIBEL ISLAND LIGHTHOUSE, EAST END OF SANIBEL ISLAND. Sanibel Island sits in an east-westerly direction among the north-south running barrier islands on Florida's Gulf Coast, where, in 1884, a 98-foot skeleton light tower was erected on the eastern tip of the island. A third-order Fresnel lens was housed in the lantern room with a fixed white light. The main column of the tower stopped about 20 feet from the ground, providing access only through an external stairway attached to the gridwork. In 1919, the murder of an assistant lighthouse keeper, Richard Barry, was committed by Jesse Lee for having insulted his wife without apologizing and then claiming self-defense. By 1923, the dwellings used for the keepers and their families were modernized with indoor plumbing and covered porches. By 1946, a hurricane left major erosion around the lighthouse, leaving one of the dwellings standing in water.

Sanibel Island. The light tower was automated in 1949, and the keepers' dwellings became home to a National Wildlife Reserve, with the Coast Guard still maintaining the light. In September 2022, Hurricane Ian, a Category 4 storm, swept through the island and took out the two keepers' dwellings, making it look like they had never been there in the first place, along with one of the main support legs for the tower. In January 2024, contractors worked to replace the temporary wood support that had been added after the hurricane with a permanent cast-iron replica of the original support column, and repairs to the stairway were also completed at that time. Within a two-week span in September and October 2024, two more hurricanes, Helene and Milton, required much cleanup once again around the light.

PORT BOCA GRANDE LIGHTHOUSE, GASPARILLA ISLAND. On the southern end of Gasparilla Island, an island roughly 10 square miles, a lighthouse was constructed on iron screw piles, with a wooden, square-shaped house and a central tower on the cupola roof, in 1890. Painted white, with a black lantern room, the lighthouse housed a third-order Fresnel lens. A short distance away from the light, an identical dwelling was constructed without the light tower for the assistant keepers and their families. The lighthouse was built 200 feet from the water, but with the constant erosion, by the 1960s, the water had encroached to 20 feet from the dwellings. To stop this erosion, the Boca Grande Conservation Council was formed to save the lighthouse.

GASPARILLA ISLAND REAR RANGE LIGHTHOUSE, GASPARILLA ISLAND. In 1927, with the importance of the shipping lanes, additional aid was needed at the island, and the Gasparilla Island Rear Range Lighthouse was constructed as an iron-pile structure to the north of the Boca Grande Light. The term "rear range" refers to the twin lights, with the rear light above the front light. A ship will be in the mid-channel when one light appears to be directly above the other light. In 1985, both the island lights were turned over to the Florida Park Service. In 2016, the lighthouse was licensed to the Barrier Island Park Society to raise funds for restoration. Still in service today, it is now known as the Gasparilla Island Lighthouse.

Gasparilla Lighthouse, Boca Grande, Florida

U. S. Light House, Boca Grande, Fla.

Light House, Pensacola, Florida.

P. & B.

PENSACOLA LIGHTHOUSE, PENSACOLA BAY. In 1858, on a 40-foot bluff at the north side of the entrance to Pensacola Bay, a brick conical-shaped tower with a granite foundation was built to a height of 150 feet, with a first-order lens in the lantern room. During the Civil War in 1861, Florida seceded from the United States, with the Confederates taking control and discontinuing the light. Later in the year, a two-day artillery battle started with half a dozen shells hitting the tower. The Union gained control of the light in 1862, and a fourth-order Fresnel lens was placed in the lantern room when it was found. The tower was still in good condition, with none of the artillery rounds having penetrated the walls.

Light House, Pensacola, Fla.

Pensacola Light. In 1869, the original first-order lens was reinstalled in the lantern room. A new keepers' dwelling was constructed that same year. The tower also got a new daymark when the bottom third of the tower was painted white, and the top portion of the tower was painted black to stand out against the cloudy sky. Because of a faulty lightning rod, the tower was hit by lightning in 1874 and 1875, and 1886 saw the tower shaken by a rare earthquake. The US Coast Guard took possession of the light when it was electrified in 1939. The lighthouse staff were removed from the light when full automation took place in 1965. The light sits on the grounds of the naval air station.

ANCLOTE KEYS LIGHTHOUSE, TARPON SPRINGS. A skeletal, cast-iron, square pyramidal tower was constructed in 1887 with four columns that slope upward toward the lantern room and support the central cylinder with its spiral staircase. A revolving third-order Fresnel lens was originally used in the lantern room. Two square clapboard-covered keepers' dwellings on elevated eight-foot piers were built because of concerns about flooding. The dwellings with large overhangs to protect from the sun were painted white, while the light tower had a brown coat of paint, and the lantern room was solid black. The light was automated in 1952 and discontinued by 1984. After the light was abandoned, the major deterioration started until a number of various groups came together to restore the lighthouse and bring it back to service again.

Crooked River Lighthouse, Carrabelle. In 1895, a 103-foot, wrought-iron, square pyramidal, skeletal tower with a central cylinder to access the lantern room with a concrete foundation was built. The lantern room housed a fourth-order bivalve lens, one that revolved on a pool of mercury that produced two white flashes every 10 seconds. Two cottages were built, with one on each side of the tower for the head keeper and his assistants. It was red until 1902, when the bottom half of the tower was painted all white to stand out against the pine forest that the tower was set in. The station became electrified in 1933 and became fully automated by 1952. The bivalve lens was used until 1976 and then removed due to leakage of mercury. The Carrabelle Lighthouse Association took over the lease for the light and helped toward its restoration.

St. Marks Lighthouse, Apalachee Bay. By 1828, the port of St. Marks at the mouth of the St. Marks River on Apalachee Bay was recognized as important to the maritime industry in that area. It had only been 10 years since the Spanish had transferred St. Marks to the United States. Constructed in 1831 of stone and brick, the tower had a height of 65 feet. With the concern of beach erosion as early as 1842, a new lighthouse was built farther inland. Built on a foundation of limestone, the walls were four feet thick at the bottom and tapered to a thickness of 18 inches near the lantern room. Having withstood hurricanes and the Civil War, a fourth-order Fresnel lens was installed along with a new keepers' dwelling by 1871. The light was automated in 1960 and is now part of the St. Marks National Wildlife Refuge.

Cedar Key Lighthouse, Seahorse Key. The Cedar Keys form a chain of barrier islands containing marshes, rivers, and creeks that have remained almost totally in their primitive state. Pres. Millard Fillmore used an executive order in 1851 to use Seahorse Key for the purpose of constructing a lighthouse. A square dwelling constructed on an elevated mound of ground, it had a hipped roofline and a staircase that led to the lantern room with its fourth-order Fresnel lens. The lighthouse saw the trouble of the Civil War and the effects of the Charleston earthquake in 1886. Pres. Herbert Hoover created the Cedar Keys National Wildlife Refuge using 13 of these barrier islands in 1929. In 2024, the Hurricanes Helene and Milton proved to be the biggest test for the Cedar Key Lighthouse.

S. T. WHITE SEA HORSE LIGHT HOUSE, CEDAR KEY, FLA.

Egmont Key Lighthouse, Tampa Bay. Constructed along Florida's Gulf Coast in 1858, this second lighthouse was moved 90 feet farther inland than the original light and rose to a height of 85 feet with a tapered cylindrical tower. The lantern room housed a third-order Fresnel lens. When the Civil War started, the light fell under Union control and was relit with a makeshift light after the Fresnel lens was removed by the lightkeeper who was sympathetic to the Confederates. After the war, thc light was replaced with a fourth-order lens. A two-story framed structure to be used as an assistant keepers' dwelling was constructed in 1899 and included a parlor, dining area, and kitchen with bedrooms both upstairs and downstairs.

EGMONT KEY. The head keepers' home was updated in 1899, and brick walkways were set in place between the dwellings, tower, and wharf. Fort Dade was constructed on the island in 1898 during the Spanish-American War as part of a coastal defense system to keep watch of the Tampa Bay area. The fort was used throughout World War I before being deactivated in 1923. By 1944, the upper portion of the lighthouse was removed, along with its Fresnel lens, and a rotating beacon was placed on top of the newly capped tower. During these times, the keepers' dwelling was demolished and replaced with one-story barracks. Egmont Key became a national wildlife refuge, with the US Fish and Wildlife Service maintaining the area. (Below, courtesy of Florida State Parks.)

American Shoal Lighthouse, Southeast of Saddlebunch Keys. Near the Looe Key, in 1880, a screw-pile-platform skeleton tower, constructed out of wrought iron, was built to a height of 110 feet. The foundation consisted of nine iron piles with one central pile surrounded by eight piles arranged in an octagon, and they were sunk 10 feet into the reef, where a two-story, eight-sided dwelling was constructed. The light was deactivated in 2015.

Charlotte Harbor Lighthouse, Punta Gorda. On the south end of Gasparilla Island is the entrance to Charlotte Harbor, where, in 1890, a screw-pile lighthouse was constructed. When finished, the light was a square, white, one-story structure with a brown roof. It housed a fifth-order Fresnel lens. In 1900, the oil house was built under the keepers' dwelling, and at that time, repairs were made to the structure. By 1943, the tower was destroyed.

Cape St. George Lighthouse, St. George Island. In 1852, a third lighthouse was built on St. George Island, this one 250 yards inland from the other lighthouses that were attempted. The tapered cylindrical tower with its balcony and lantern room was constructed using as much salvage from the previously destroyed lights as possible. The foundation would be made up of a ring of pine pilings driven into the sand and stone. Cape St. George made it through the Civil War with little disturbances, unlike many of the other southern lights. In 1949, the station was automated, and a bridge was built in 1965 to connect the island to the mainland. Erosion of the beach area around the tower carried on, and with the help of Hurricane Andrew in 1992 and Hurricane Opal in 1995, the tower settled into the sand. (Above, courtesy of the US Coast Guard.)

St. Joseph Point Lighthouse, Port St. Joe. St. Joseph Point Lighthouse was built on the northern tip of the peninsula, where the old St. Joseph Bay Lighthouse once stood, on one of the best natural harbors along the Gulf Coast at St. Joseph Bay. In 1902, a one-story frame building was constructed on brick piers approximately eight feet off the ground. Within the walls were five rooms and a watch room over the center of the building with an iron lantern room housing the third-order Fresnel lens. During World War II, the men of the US Coast Guard used the watch room to look out for the enemy and used the area beneath the building as a barracks. The light was deactivated in 1960 and soon sold into private ownership.

St. Johns River Light, Jacksonville. In 1858, a lighthouse was constructed here after two previous attempts were made in 1830 and 1834. The light, one mile inland, was built of brick, stood 74 feet tall, and housed a fixed third-order Fresnel lens in the lantern room. Shortly after its construction, the Civil War broke out, and the lighthouse remained in operation through much of the war until 1864, when a Confederate sympathizer shot the light out. By 1867, the light was relit with a third-order lens. The 1886 earthquake centered in Charleston, South Carolina, was felt at St. Johns River Light, but it suffered no damage. By 1929, the lightship *Brunswick*, which was stationed off the coast of Georgia, was renamed the *St. Johns* and reassigned approximately seven miles off the coast from the St. Johns River. The lighthouse was then decommissioned in 1931. (Below, courtesy of Kraig Anderson and lighthousefriends.com.)

Cape San Blas Lighthouse, Port St. Joe. Sitting in the southernmost point of Florida's panhandle, three previous lighthouses were used to light the area before the last attempt was made in 1885. This fourth skeleton tower had four iron legs that ran the length of the tower with a network of iron braces and a central column housing the spiral staircase. Two keepers' dwellings were also erected at the same time. In the past, the erosion of the beach area had brought down the previous lights, and the new one was in danger of quitting soon after its first lighting. A 1916 hurricane eroded much of the beach area, and the light was temporarily discontinued in 1918. With this being part of the Coastal Barrier Resources Area, which does not allow beach renourishment projects, the Cape San Blas Lighthouse was added to the official "Doomsday List," and the only solution to save this light is to move it, at a very costly price. Now, a sign on the lighthouse reads, "Move It or Lose It."

Seven

The Gulf States

Choctaw Point Lighthouse, Mobile Bay, Alabama. In 1826, the Mobile Channel was opened up, giving the city of Mobile more shipping traffic. By 1830, a brick lighthouse was constructed on Choctaw Point in an area that protruded from the west side of the shore just south of town. It was not until 1854 that its daymark would be its whitewashed color. In November 1862, during the Civil War, the light was extinguished by the Confederate forces. Because of obstructions placed in the channel during the war, the light was never relit. (Courtesy of *Lighthouse Digest*.)

BATTERY GLADDEN LIGHTHOUSE, MOBILE BAY, ALABAMA. When changes in the Mobile Channel took place after the Civil War, a screw-pile lighthouse was erected to replace the old Choctaw Point Light and placed on the west side of the mouth of the Mobile River. Built on five wrought iron screw piles, the framed dwelling carried a center tower with a lantern room housing a fourth-order lantern. It was built on an artificial island that Confederate forces constructed to protect the city of Mobile. The light was extinguished in 1913 and used as a daymark for shipping, but by 1950, it succumbed to the elements of weather. (Both, courtesy of National Archives.)

MIDDLE BAY (MOBILE BAY) LIGHTHOUSE, MOBILE BAY, ALABAMA. In the center of Mobile Bay, in 1885, a screw-pile lighthouse was constructed with a wooden hexagonal dwelling hosting a pyramidal roof that had a slope upward to a lantern room in the center of the structure. It was supported by seven legs, with a single leg extension extending from each corner and a center leg, and they were screwed to the bottom of the bay. The lantern room housed a fourth-order Fresnel lens. Its daymark was the dwelling, painted white, with a black lantern room and red foundation piles. By 1905, the lantern was removed, and two acetylene lights were mounted on the structure; it continues to be an active light.

Fort Morgan Sand Island Lighthouse, Sand Island, Alabama. The third light tower to be constructed on Sand Island was built in 1873 as a 132-foot, tapered cylindrical brick tower with a lantern room housing a second-order lens, offering a visibility of 17.5 miles. At the same time, a two-story keepers' dwelling was also constructed for both head and assistant keepers. By 1881, the tower was coated in tar, giving it a black daymark. The tower was built on a 12-foot-thick concrete foundation with the support of 170 timber piles. By 1885, with the erosion of the island, brush and stone jetties were used along the shoreline, but shortly, storms damaged the jetties, as the shoreline was only 10 feet from the lighthouse. (Left, courtesy of the US Coast Guard.)

FORT MORGAN. In 1893, the keepers' dwelling was moved 750 feet from the tower area to escape the continuing erosion. Over the ensuing years, tons of riprap, oyster shells, and rocks were used to hold the water back from the lighthouse. The keepers' dwelling was demolished in a hurricane in 1906, and soon, the base of the tower became the living quarter for the keepers. It is believed that some 25,000 tons of rock have been used to stop or hold back the erosion. The working conditions around the lighthouse continued to become more dangerous, as keepers would need rowboats in the wrought waters to just get to the light. The lighthouse was deactivated in 1933, but restoration efforts to save the light continue today.

MOBILE POINT LIGHTHOUSE, BALDWIN COUNTY, ALABAMA. There were a series of range lights at the entrance to Mobile Bay, near the Fort Morgan peninsular. Built in 1822 as a concrete conical tower 49 feet tall, the Mobile Point Light was added to the series of range lights. After Sand Island was added to the area in 1858, the Mobile Point Light was downgraded to a fourth-order Fresnel lens. During the Battle of Mobile Bay during the Civil War, cannon fire all but destroyed one side of the lighthouse. (Both, courtesy of the National Park Service.)

8th Dist. 37-3 Mobile Pt. Lt. Sta. Ala.

A

From 80' S.W.

B

From 300' S.S.W. of Tower.

Filed 11-18-14

Taken 9-17-1914

Cat Island Lighthouse, Cat Island, Mississippi. The first Cat Island Lighthouse was a brick, conical, 30-foot tower built in 1831. It was built on sand, and with the constant shore erosion, hurricane damage in 1860, and damage from the Confederate forces during the Civil War, a new light was soon needed. In 1871, a square iron screw-pile lighthouse with a lantern room housing a fifth-order Fresnel lens was constructed. Due to lessening shipping traffic, the lighthouse was discontinued in 1937. After years of neglect, a fire burned the light to the ground in 1961.

SHIP ISLAND LIGHTHOUSE, FORT MASSACHUSETTS, MISSISSIPPI. Because of its deep harbor, the first light tower built at Ship Island was in 1853. The tower was constructed of brick and used lamps and reflectors as its light source. In 1861, the Confederates took over the island with its partially finished fort, and after a skirmish with the Union ship the *Massachusetts*, they abandoned the island—but not before setting the lighthouse tower on fire. In 1886, with the old tower having been condemned, a new 62-foot, square, wooden, open-framed lighthouse was constructed with a lantern room, housing the lens from the original light. Always concerned with beach erosion, the bricks from the old tower were used to build a jetty to help with the erosion around the tower.

Ship Island. In 1929, the tower saw a lightning strike during a storm but only suffered minimal damage. Electricity from a kerosene generator and battery was installed in 1930. The US Coast Guard manned the lighthouse until 1949, when the station was fully automated. The lighthouse was put up for sale in 1965 on the condition that the tower was moved from the property, and with one bidder, the light sold for $250 but was never moved. Ship Island was cut in half when Hurricane Camille hit the island in 1969, creating an East Ship Island and West Ship Island and leaving the tower damaged. In June 1972, a neglected campfire and high winds spread to the lighthouse, and it burned to the ground.

LIGHTHOUSE ON SHIP ISLAND

BILOXI LIGHTHOUSE, BILOXI, MISSISSIPPI. Mississippi representative Jefferson Davis, in 1847, authorized one of the first cast-iron truncated cone-shaped lighthouses in the South to be placed in the city of Biloxi. In 1856, a fourth-order Fresnel lens replaced the lamps and reflectors used to that point. An 1860 storm damaged a good portion of the seawall and the foundation under the light tower, resulting in a two-foot leaning from its vertical position. When the Civil War started in 1861, the light was extinguished, and the keys to the light tower were seized by the "Home Guard."

Biloxi Light. The restoration work on the tower started after the war by relocating the soil under the opposite side from the lean so the light would right itself to the vertical position. Both the tower and the keepers' dwelling were painted white after a poor attempt at painting the tower black in hopes of warding off any rust, for a short time, between 1866 and 1868. By 1939, as with most other lighthouses, the responsibility of the tower came under the US Coast Guard. Deeded to the City of Biloxi in 1968, the light would open to the public. Hurricane Katrina hit the 64-foot light tower, and many of the inside bricks were dislodged, and windows were broken.

Merrill's Shell Bank Lighthouse, Pass Christian, Mississippi. The Pass Marian Lighthouse, as it was originally called, helped sailing ships steer clear of the Mississippi Sound's shallow waters. After using a revenue cutter lightship to light the western tip of Cat Island from 1847 onward, the first screw pile, built in 1859, had a wooden keepers' dwelling with a lantern room 45 feet above sea level. Confederate troops during the Civil War put the lighthouse out of commission until the Union forces relit the light in 1863. The lighthouse suffered only minor damage during that time. In 1883, the lighthouse structure caught fire and was completely destroyed. Shortly after, a new lighthouse was constructed on the original piles that had escaped the blaze. In 1944, the Victorian-style keepers' dwelling was torn down with the replacement of a skeleton tower once again using the original pilings. (Courtesy of the US Coast Guard.)

Sabine Pass Lighthouse, Cameron Parish, Louisiana. Sabine Pass Lighthouse stands in southwest Louisiana, where the Sabine and Neches Rivers meet. This brick octagon lighthouse was constructed in 1856 and features eight large buttresses at its base that help to stabilize the heavy structure. The light was extinguished at the start of the Civil War to prevent Union ships from using it as a guide into the rivers. The lighthouse was relit after the war in 1865. The US Coast Guard deactivated the light in 1952. A fire destroyed most of the outbuildings in 1972, including the keepers' dwellings. Since 2001, the Cameron Preservation Alliance has worked to restore the tower. In 2009, the lighthouse became part of the fifth series of lighthouse stamps the US Postal Service brought out to honor these lights.

NEW CANAL LIGHTHOUSE, NEW ORLEANS, LOUISIANA. At the north end of the New Basin Canal in 1838, an octagonal wooden tower lighthouse with a foundation of wood pilings was constructed near the city of New Orleans, which lies near the shore of Lake Pontchartrain and the Mississippi River. Early on, Irish and German immigrants helped construct this canal from the Lake Pontchartrain area. When first lit, oil lamps and reflectors were used to produce a fixed white light. By 1855, a second New Canal Lighthouse was constructed as a square, one-story structure using iron pilings. The lighthouses had a four-sided sloping roofline with a lantern room on top, housing a fifth-order Fresnel lens. Although the Union forces took New Orleans in 1862, the light had been active until then. It was relit after the war.

A 16607 Light House, West End, New Orleans, La.

New Canal Light. In 1890, after the lighthouse was sold at a private auction, a new, two-story lighthouse was built on an iron-pile foundation and painted white with a black lantern room. It now had a 49-foot focal plane so as to be seen at a great range. With landfill projects in the early 1900s, the 1,000-foot leeway it originally had brought the shore closer to the lighthouse. The lighthouse saw hurricanes in 1903, 1915, 1926, and 1927, but Hurricane Katrina in 2005 heavily damaged the lighthouse beyond repair, even after the concrete piles were added in 1927 and the filing in with earth under the lighthouse in 1936. The Lake Pontchartrain Basin Foundation came in, salvaged the historical materials, and reopened the lighthouse as a museum in 2013.

PORT PONTCHARTRAIN LIGHTHOUSE, NEW ORLEANS, LOUISIANA. In 1855, a concrete slab was laid on the lake bottom supported by piles 2,100 feet from the shoreline, where a conical brick lighthouse was constructed. The lantern room used lamps and reflectors until 1857, when a fifth-order Fresnel lens was put in place. After the Civil War, the old, original, weather-boarded pyramid lighthouse was taken apart, and the wood was used to build a walkway over the lake to the railroad pier. The light was discontinued in 1929. Often used by locals to shelter from hurricanes, the lighthouse became part of the Pontchartrain Beach Amusement Park in 1939. (Below, courtesy of the National Archives.)

Point Au Fer Reef Lighthouse, Atchafalaya Bay, Louisiana. The Atchafalaya Entrance Channel is where, in 1913, a lighthouse with a foundation of 25 iron-cased piles was constructed for the 32-foot square platform. A square wooden tower on a one-and-a-half-story keepers' house was painted white with an all-black lantern room using a fourth-order Fresnel lens. The light was deactivated in 1975 and replaced by a skeleton-style tower. The US Coast Guard offered the deactivated lighthouse to various groups, but when no takers came, the Coast Guard set fire to the lighthouse, and it burned to the ground. (Below, courtesy of the US Coast Guard.)

West Rigolets Lighthouse, Rigolets Bayou, Louisiana. The West Rigolets Lighthouse was constructed as part of a set of four lighthouses used to protect the area around Lake Pontchartrain in 1855. Built as a square dwelling with a hipped roof and a circular lantern room, the light was deactivated in 1945 and destroyed by Hurricane Katrina in 2005. (Courtesy of the US Coast Guard.)

Cubits Gap Lighthouse, Cubits Gap, Louisiana. On the northeastern side of the Mississippi River and the southeastern side of Cubits Gap, a lighthouse was established in 1891. This light was in the form of a fog-signal tower at a height of 30 feet, constructed as a square wooden tower built on piles with a white-painted daymark. The light became automated in 1961. (Courtesy of the US Coast Guard.)

Brazos Santiago Pass, Texas. The dividing line between Texas and Mexico is the Rio Grande, but with the shallowness of the river, only smaller ships could use it to off-load goods. The US Army recommended that because of the increase in maritime shipping through the Brazos Santiago Pass to Port Isabell and the increase in the foggy conditions in the area, a lighthouse should be constructed. Pres. Zachary Taylor signed the bill for the appropriation of $15,000 to build the lighthouse and beacon light in 1850. An 82-foot brick tower was soon constructed with a stationary white light seen for 15 miles. (Below, courtesy of the Library of Congress.)

POINT ISABEL LIGHTHOUSE, PORT ISABEL, TEXAS. It was 1853 before the 82-foot tower was first lit using 15 lamps and reflectors in the lantern room. In 1857, a third-order Fresnel lens was put into use. The lighthouse became deactivated during the years of the Civil War. During the war, federal ships blockaded the Texas coast, but the lighthouse was occupied by both Confederate and Union soldiers over the course of the war. The tower was eventually hit by cannon fire and damaged. After the lens was removed for safety's sake, the lantern room was used as a watch tower by both sides. When the Confederates were retreating, the light was again in danger from the exploding powder that was left in the tower, causing considerable damage.

Point Isabell Lookout. The lighthouse required repair when the Union forces regained the light, but it was not until after the war in 1866 that it was accomplished. By 1897, the tower was in a dilapidated condition and in need of repair because of leaks to the lantern room. A new lantern room was installed in 1881. Originally, the Lighthouse Board never secured the property with a title when the first light was constructed, so rather than pay the owner of the land, the lighthouse was discontinued in 1888. In 1895, Congress finally allocated the funds to pay the owner, and the light was once again turned on. The light would operate for an additional 10 years until it was deactivated in 1905. It was sold at auction in 1927 to a private owner.

THE TEXAS STATE PARK BOARD. After lying unused for most of the first half of the century, in 1950, the Texas State Park Board stepped in to help with the restoration of the lighthouse. Using original descriptions, the outside of the lighthouse was recovered with plaster, and the original iron lantern platform was replaced with concrete. A mercury-vapor lamp was installed in the tower, with it once again aiding the maritime traffic. Today, it stands as a beacon for the Texas State Historical Park and a functioning navigational aid for the maritime traffic of the area. It is one of the oldest still-functioning lighthouses on the Texas Gulf Coast.

Aransas Pass Lighthouse Station, Harbor Island, Texas. The Aransas Pass Light became one of a number of stations built in 1857 by the lighthouse service in the Aransas Pass-Corpus Christi area. A keepers' dwelling and a brick tower painted brown were built to a height of 54 feet and housed a lantern room with a fourth-order Fresnel lens. During the Civil War, the Confederates tried to destroy the light by blowing off the top 20 feet of the tower. After the war, the damaged light and tower were repaired. With hurricanes in the ensuing years, the keepers' dwelling was swept away, and damage to the tower repairs were continual. In 1955, the Aransas Pass Lighthouse was sold to a private owner.

BOLIVAR POINT LIGHTHOUSE, PORT BOLIVAR, TEXAS. In 1852, on the western end of Bolivar Point at the entrance to Galveston Bay, a 65-foot tower was constructed from iron sections of metal. The keepers' dwelling was constructed at the same time while work was being done on the tower itself. Lamps and reflectors were housed in the lantern room, but soon the brightness, or lack of it, became an issue, and a third-order Fresnel lens was added. The height of the tower needed more iron sections added to it, and that was carried out in 1858. Within three years, the Civil War made it necessary to dismantle the iron sections and use them to help the war effort. After the war, a new 117-foot tower was constructed with iron sections, and a third-order Fresnel lens was used to provide light.

Bolivar Point. By 1882, a more powerful lens was needed, so a second-order lens was used to help with the mariners' complaints of the dimness of the tower. The daymark given to the light was broad horizontal bands of black and white. The Great Hurricane of 1900 swamped Galveston with five feet of water, killing as many as 6,000 people and all but destroying the city. About 120 people sought protection, and they hoped the lighthouse could provide it. There, they waited out the 120-mile-an-hour winds. In 1915, sixty people sought shelter in the tower, and all the buildings and fences outside of the tower were wiped away. Accidentally used for target practice in 1917 by the military, a couple of projectiles penetrated the tower. The lighthouse was transferred over to the War Department in 1935, and the War Assets Administration sold the property to a private owner in 1947.

Brazos Santiago Lighthouse, Padre Island, Texas. This light sits on the Texas coast just before reaching the Mexican boundary. A new wooden lighthouse, constructed in 1854, replaced the moveable structure on wheels that originally lit the area. The tower was replaced again in 1864 after its destruction during the Civil War. By 1872, it became known that, once again, a replacement needed to be considered. In 1874, the lighthouse was hit by a major hurricane; the wooden tower was swept out to sea, and the station was destroyed, along with the unfortunate death of the keeper's wife.

BRAZOS SANTIAGO. A temporary beacon was established while the next light was being constructed. In 1879, a new tower was built as a wooden, cottage-style, screw-pile lighthouse. Parts of this light came from Philadelphia in the way of the metal piling and ironworks, and the framed dwelling portion was from Mobile. Little more is known of this light until 1940, when a painting crew accidentally set fire to the building, just leaving the metal screw piles in place. After that, a lens was put on top of the nearby US Coast Guard building.

Halfmoon Reef Lighthouse, Port Lavaca, Texas. In 1854, Congress approved funds to build a screw-pile lighthouse on the south tip of Matagorda Bay. The light was supported by seven 25-foot iron pilings. A wooden dwelling, 16 feet on each side of the hexagon, had a lantern room that housed a sixth-order Fresnel lens. Having been moved to land in 1943, it now welcomes visitors to Port Lavaca on land instead of at sea.

Brazos River Lighthouse, Velasco, Texas. Located at the entrance to the Brazos River in the Gulf of Mexico, in 1896, the tower was completed. It was a skeleton iron tower with a central cylinder housing stairs, It was painted a brown color with a black lantern room that housed a third-order Fresnel lens. A new structure was built after the hurricane of 1900, when the station was totally destroyed. The tower was dismantled in 1967. (Courtesy of the National Archives.)

GALVESTON JETTY (SOUTH JETTY) LIGHTHOUSE, GALVESTON BAY, TEXAS. In 1904, work began on placing nine wrought-iron pilings on the seabed near the end of the south jetty. Then, 200 tons of rock ballast were placed around the pilings to secure them to the jetty. Metal beams formed the skeleton as well as the support platform at 42 feet above the water line. The structure housed the workings of the light, with a floor above used for living quarters for the head keeper and the assistant. The structure was not yet complete when the hurricane of 1915 struck the Galveston area. The light got off with only minor repairs needed. A third-order Fresnel lens was placed in the tower in 1917. The light was delayed in being activated because of a coastal blackout during World War I. The lighthouse fell into the sea after a violent storm in 2000.

Fort Point Lighthouse, Galveston Bay, Texas. Built on the northeast end of Galveston Island in 1882, a screw-pile lighthouse was constructed. The screw-pile lighthouses were equipped with two floors that combined both the keepers' living quarters and lantern room, all sitting atop iron pilings fixed into the shallow waters beneath them. By 1909, the Fort Point Lighthouse was discontinued. (Courtesy of the US Coast Guard.)

Red Fish Bar Lighthouse, Galveston Bay, Texas. In 1853, Red Fish Bar was under construction as a screw-pile-style lighthouse to work in cooperation with Fort Point Light and Halfmoon Shoal Light. After the Civil War, the only portion left of the light was the iron screw piles it had been attached to, but repairs were completed by 1869. Damaged in a fire in 1900, the light was replaced with an eight-day lantern. (Courtesy of the US Coast Guard.)

Resources

lighthousefriends.com
uslhs.org
uslhs.org, Chesapeake Chapter
uslhs.org/resources/keepers-log, The Keepers Log, Fall 1991
www.archives.gov
www.dhs.gov
www.lighthousedigest.com
www.loc.gov
www.uscg.mil